Contents

The Journey Begins

The Fagbemi family live in Tottenham, North London. Today they are going on a day trip to Brighton. Most of their journey will be by train.

The family leave home at 9 o'clock in the morning.

Scotland

England

Wales

Tottenham

London

Brighton

This map shows where Tottenham and Brighton are in Britain.

The family walk to Tottenham Hale Underground station. They use a **street map** to find their way.

This street map shows the **route** to the station.

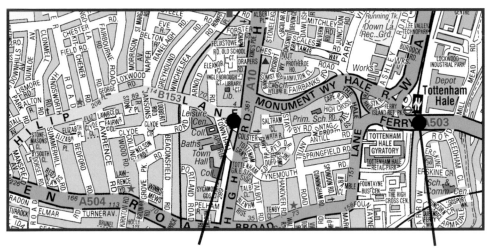

The family home is here.   The station is here.

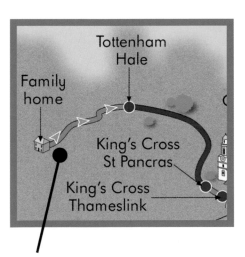

The pink line shows that the family walk to the station.

To the left is part of a route map that follows the family's journey. Through each section of the book it shows the places they pass by and how they travel. It does not show the actual distance between places or the exact route they travel along.

Look out for extra maps that give other information about the route and what the family see.

Crossing London

Time: 35 minutes. Distance so far: 12 km.

Inside the station, the family look at a **London Underground** Tube map to work out their route to King's Cross St Pancras by train.

Tottenham is about 10 km from King's Cross.

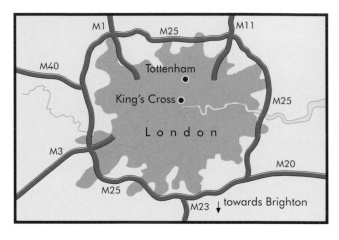

The Tube map shows all the Underground stations and the lines that connect them. Like the route map opposite, it is not a **scale** map. It does not help people above ground to find their way.

To get to King's Cross St Pancras the family go south on the Victoria line.

At 9.30 am, the family arrive at King's Cross St Pancras. They walk to another station nearby, called King's Cross Thameslink. This is where they must catch their train to Brighton.

Outside King's Cross St Pancras, the London streets are very busy with traffic.

The red line shows the family's journey on the Underground.

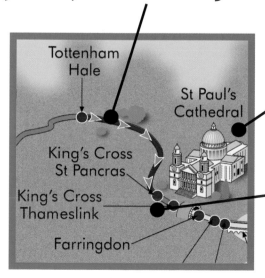

The brown background shows that this is a **built-up area**.

The pink line shows that they walk from King's Cross St Pancras to King's Cross Thameslink.

Leaving the City

Time: 1 hour 24 minutes. Distance so far: 33 km.

The family wait on the platform at King's Cross Thameslink station.

Look at the Thameslink route map on the right. It is similar to the London Underground map. It is the only map the family need for this part of the journey.

The train's route to Brighton is the dark blue line. The train began its journey in Bedford. The family catch the train at King's Cross Thameslink. How many stations do they have to pass through before reaching Brighton?

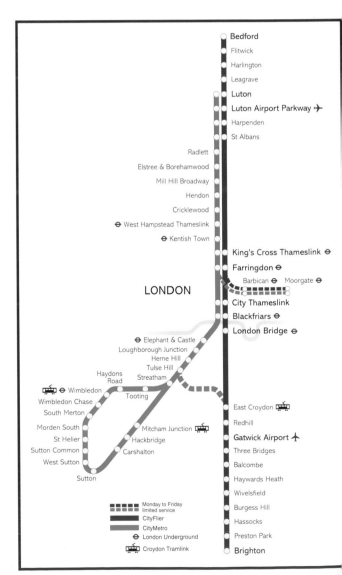

Bedford
Flitwick
Harlington
Leagrave
Luton
Luton Airport Parkway ✈
Harpenden
St Albans
Radlett
Elstree & Borehamwood
Mill Hill Broadway
Hendon
Cricklewood
⊖ West Hampstead Thameslink
⊖ Kentish Town

King's Cross Thameslink ⊖
Farringdon ⊖
Barbican ⊖ Moorgate ⊖

LONDON

City Thameslink ⊖
Blackfriars ⊖
London Bridge ⊖

⊖ Elephant & Castle
Loughborough Junction
Herne Hill
Tulse Hill
Streatham
Haydons Road
Wimbledon
Wimbledon Chase
South Merton
Tooting
Morden South
Mitcham Junction
St Helier
Hackbridge
Sutton Common
Carshalton
West Sutton
Sutton

East Croydon
Redhill
Gatwick Airport ✈
Three Bridges
Balcombe
Haywards Heath
Wivelsfield
Burgess Hill
Hassocks
Preston Park
Brighton

Monday to Friday limited service
CityFlier
CityMetro
⊖ London Underground
Croydon Tramlink

When the train leaves King's Cross Thameslink, it goes through some long tunnels. After Blackfriars station, it crosses the River Thames over Blackfriars Bridge.

*The children spot some famous London **landmarks** as they cross the river. Can you spot Tower Bridge?*

The train moves out of central London. It travels along a busy stretch of track, crossing many sets of **points**.

At 10.24 am, the train pulls in at East Croydon.

Can you see where they cross the River Thames?

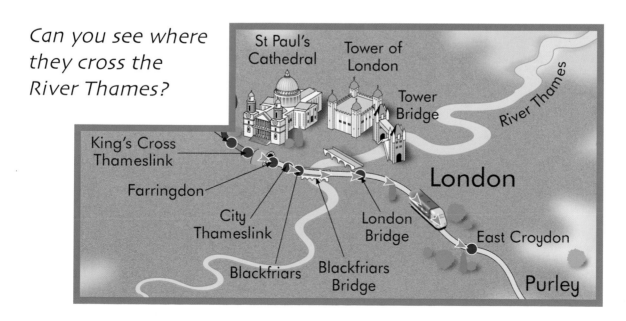

Roads and Runways

Time: 1 hour 40 minutes. Distance so far: 53 km.

After the train leaves East Croydon, it goes through several other towns. The family speed past Purley, Coulsdon and Redhill.

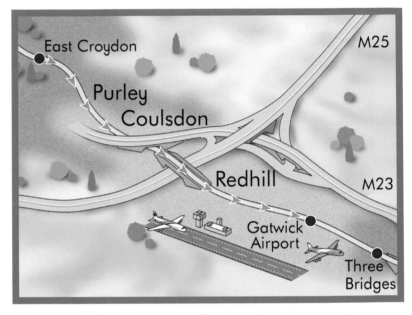

Can you see the towns the train passes?

A ticket collector inspects the family's tickets. The children look out of the windows and see gardens and trees between the houses. This area has more open space than the crowded city.

This **Ordnance Survey map** gives more information about the things the family see from the train window.

The map uses **symbols** to show where things are. The railway track is the solid black line. **Motorways** are coloured blue.

Can you see where the train goes through a tunnel under a motorway, then over another motorway on a bridge?

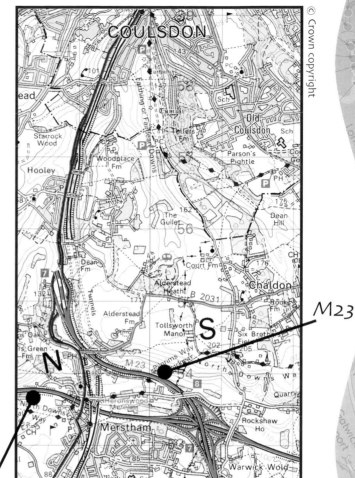

M23

M25

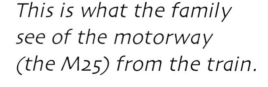

This is what the family see of the motorway (the M25) from the train.

The train arrives at Gatwick Airport station at 10.40 am. The family catch a glimpse of the **runway**.

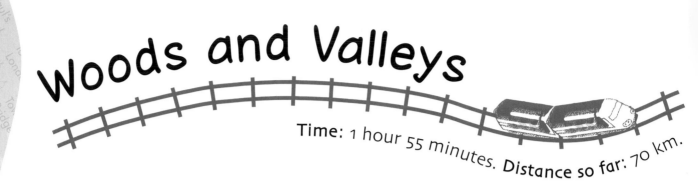

Woods and Valleys

After leaving Gatwick and the town of Crawley behind, the train enters the countryside. It passes through some woodland and a beautiful **valley**.

The family do not see much of Balcombe Forest, because the train goes through a tunnel underneath it.

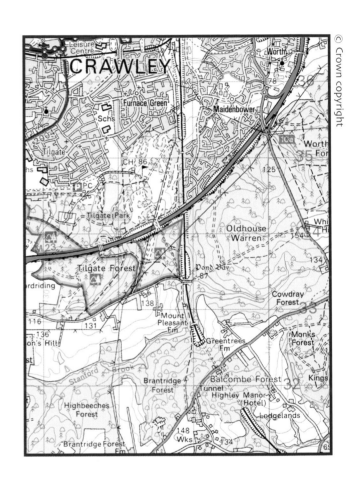

© Crown copyright

Can you find Balcombe Forest tunnel on this Ordnance Survey map? Follow the solid black train line until it becomes a dotted line running through a patch of green.

The tunnel is also shown on the map opposite, but with a different symbol. Can you find it?

*The train goes over the River Ouse on this old stone **viaduct**.*

Can you find the viaduct on this map?

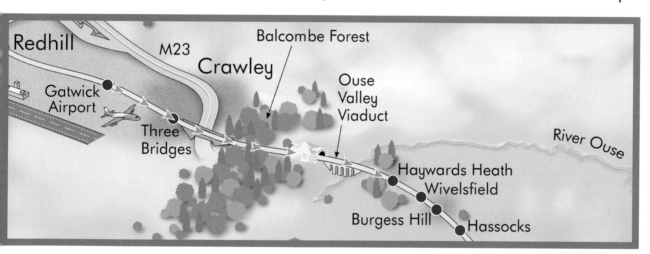

Soon the train pulls in at Haywards Heath station. It is 10.55 am and the family left London just over an hour ago. They eat some snacks and check the **timetable**.

Towards Burgess Hill

Time: 2 hours 1 minute. Distance so far: 75 km.

The train continues south towards Burgess Hill.

The family read books to pass the time.

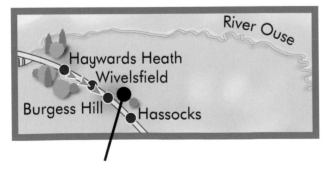

River Ouse

Haywards Heath
Wivelsfield
Burgess Hill
Hassocks

The brown area shows this is a built-up area.

When the train enters the town the family can see more houses, as this is a built-up area.

This railway bridge is next to Wivelsfield station in north Burgess Hill. Find Wivelsfield station on the map opposite.

The train arrives at Burgess Hill station at 11.01 am.

Under a Bridleway

Time: 2 hours 4 minutes. Distance so far: 78 km.

Just south of Burgess Hill, the train goes under a bridge where a **bridleway** crosses the railway track.

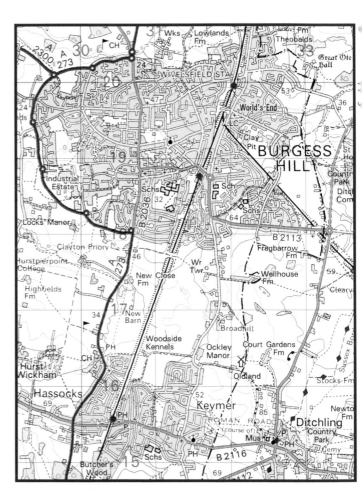

The Brighton train passes underneath this bridleway.

The bridleway is shown as a line of long pink dashes running over a bridge. Follow the black line of the railway until you find it.

The train pulls into Hassocks station.

It takes three minutes to travel from Burgess Hill to Hassocks. This stretch of track is just over 3 km long. The train has travelled at a speed of about 1 km per minute.

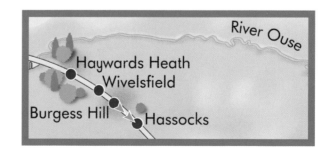

Hassocks is one stop away from Burgess Hill.

Through the Downs

Time: 2 hours 11 minutes. **Distance so far:** 85 km.

Between Hassocks and the next station, Preston Park, the countryside is very pretty.

The railway line passes a stretch of hills called the South Downs. The family do not see these hills, because the train goes through a tunnel underneath them.

Why do you think the railway line runs through a tunnel, and not over the top of these hills?

The train also goes through some **cuttings**. This is where the path for the track actually 'cuts' into high ground, so trains travel on a lower level than the hills all around.

The train enters a built-up area. The family are now in Brighton. They stop on the north side of the town, at a station called Preston Park.

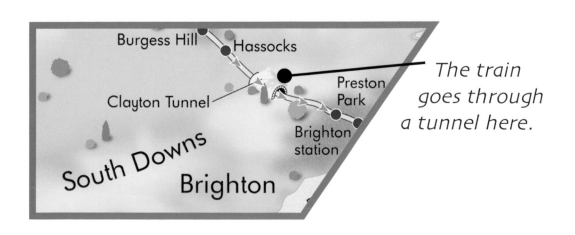

Burgess Hill   Hassocks

Clayton Tunnel

Preston Park

Brighton station

South Downs   Brighton

The train goes through a tunnel here.

Arriving in Brighton

Time: 2 hours 15 minutes. Distance so far: 87 km.

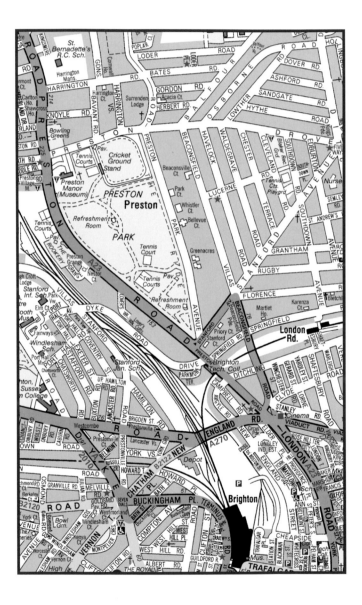

From Preston Park, it is a short distance to Brighton station.

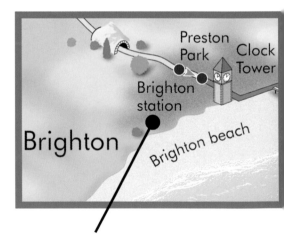

The family are back in a built-up area.

To see a town in more detail, a street map like this is useful.
The large black shape at the bottom is Brighton station.
The train arrives from the north-west side of the town.

The train comes in on time. It is 11.15 am.

When the train pulls in to Brighton station, this part of the family's journey is at an end.

They get out of their carriage and walk down the platform of the fine old **Victorian** station.

Now it's time to find the beach!

Walk to the Sea

Time: 2 hours 30 minutes. Distance so far: 89 km.

The family leave Brighton station and walk towards the sea. They buy a **tourist map** of the town to help them find the way.

This is the safest place to cross the road.

Just outside the station, the family cross Gloucester Road at some traffic lights.

This is part of the tourist map the family use. They decide to walk down Queen's Road to the Clock Tower, then down West Street to the beach. Can you follow their route on the map?

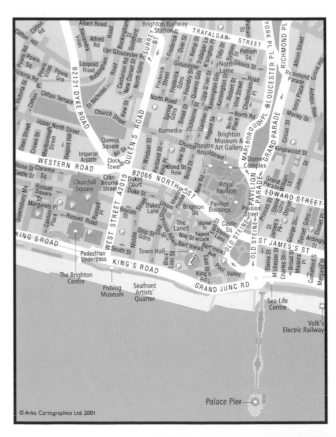

© Arka Cartographics Ltd. 2001

24

It takes the family about ten minutes to reach the seafront.

Brighton Palace Pier is a famous landmark. It can be seen from far away.

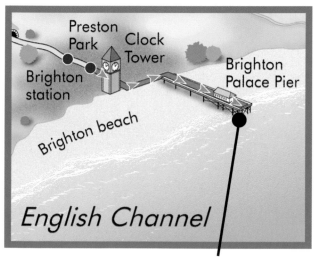

The pink line shows that the family walk to the end of the pier.

The family then continue along the **promenade** towards the **pier**. They walk right to the end of the pier to look at the view.

Follow the Map

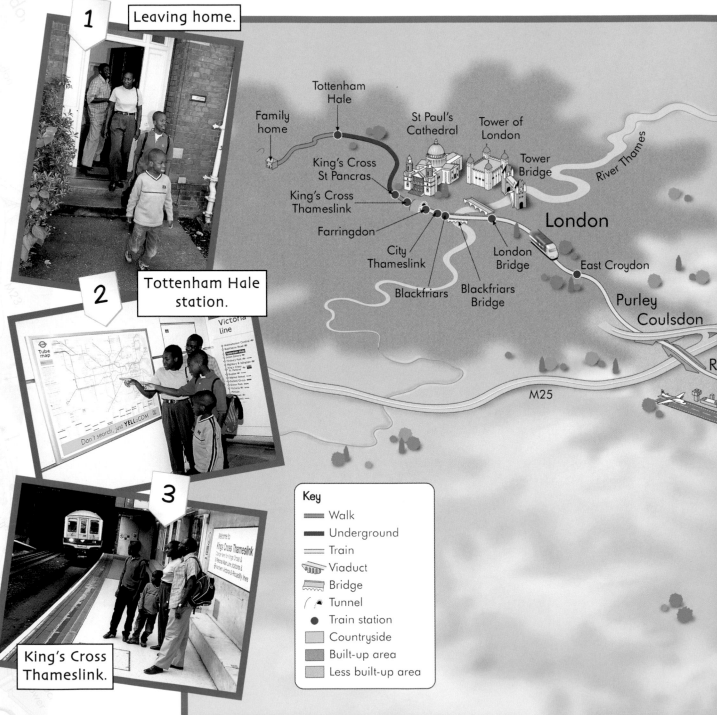

1 Leaving home.

2 Tottenham Hale station.

3 King's Cross Thameslink.

Family home

Tottenham Hale

King's Cross St Pancras

King's Cross Thameslink

Farringdon

City Thameslink

Blackfriars

Blackfriars Bridge

London Bridge

St Paul's Cathedral

Tower of London

Tower Bridge

River Thames

London

East Croydon

Purley

Coulsdon

M25

Victoria line

Welcome to King's Cross Thameslink

Key
- 🟦 Walk
- ⬛ Underground
- ⬜ Train
- 🪜 Viaduct
- 🌉 Bridge
- 🕳 Tunnel
- ⬤ Train station
- ⬜ Countryside
- ⬛ Built-up area
- ⬜ Less built-up area

The Fagbemi family have enjoyed their journey to Brighton. They travelled across London on the Underground, and had an interesting overland train ride. Here is the whole of their route. Find where each photo was taken on the map.

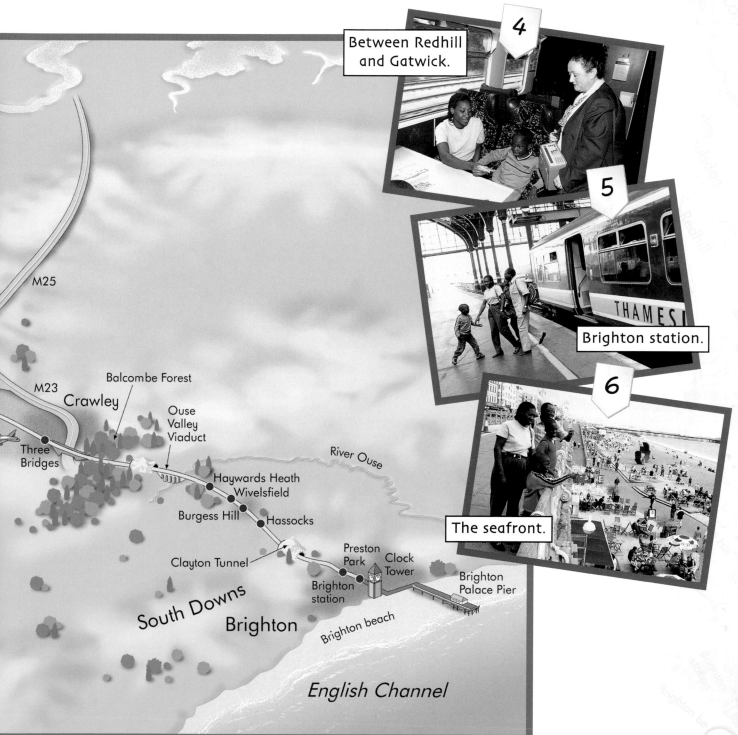

4
Between Redhill and Gatwick.

5
Brighton station.

6
The seafront.

27

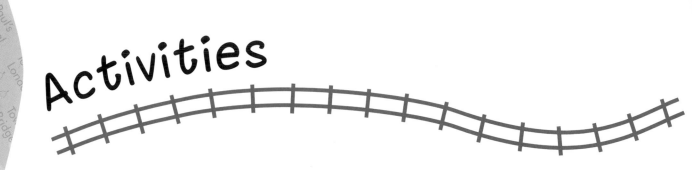

Activities

Work it Out

1. Get a copy of the London Underground Tube map. Can you work out the family's journey from Tottenham Hale to King's Cross?

2. Look at page 7. What route do you think the family take to get to the station?

3. Look at page 20. Why don't the family get a good view of the hilly countryside from the train window?

4. Look at the tourist map on page 24. Find a different route to get from the station to the Palace Pier.

5. Look at the route map on pages 26-27. What different forms of travel do the family use? What different features do they see?

Design Your Own Map

- Think about a day trip you have made. What did you pass on the way? (e.g. shops, parks, woods.)
- Design some small, clear symbols for these things.
- Draw the route and add the symbols. Use different colours for the different ways you travelled.

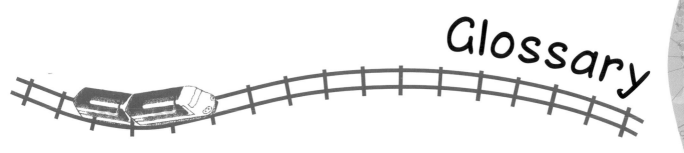

Glossary

bridleway
A path that can be used by horse-riders, cyclists and walkers.

built-up area
A place with lots of houses. An area that is less built up has fewer houses and more green areas.

cutting
A route for a railway track or road that is cut through high ground.

key
A map key explains what all the symbols on the map mean.

landmark
Something that is easy to recognise.

London Underground
A network of train lines under the streets of London, linking different places in the city. It is also called the Tube.

motorway
A fast road with at least two lanes of traffic in each direction.

Ordnance Survey map
A detailed map that gives lots of information about the features of an area.

pier
A long walkway, going out from the shore over the sea.

points
The part of a railway line where a train can change from one track to another.

promenade
A wide footpath beside a beach.

route
The way you go to get from one place to another.

runway
A stretch of tarmac used by planes for taking off and landing.

scale
The size used to show an area of land on a map, compared to the size of that land in real life.

street map
A map that names all the roads in an area.

symbol
A simple picture on a map which represents something, such as a station or a church. Symbols are explained in the key to the map.

timetable
A list of the journey times for particular trains, or other forms of transport.

tourist map
A map of an area specially designed for people visiting on holiday.

valley
Low land between hills.

viaduct
A long bridge that takes a railway or road over a valley.

Victorian
From the time when Queen Victoria reigned (1837 – 1901).

Index

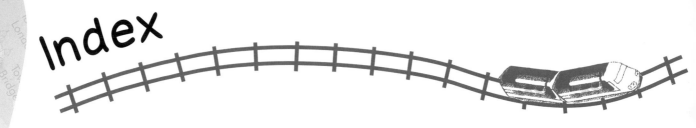

About this Book

FOLLOW THE MAP is designed as a first introduction to map skills. The series is made up of familiar journeys that the young reader is encouraged to follow. In doing so the child will begin to develop an understanding of the relation between maps and the geographical environment they describe. Here are some suggestions to gain the maximum benefit from TRAIN JOURNEY.

A variety of maps are illustrated in the book including a topological map (Thameslink map), Ordnance Survey maps, street maps and a tourist map. Discuss the differences and/or similarities between the maps. Who are they for, and why?

The train journey takes the family through a very varied landscape. Compare the urban scenes with the rural ones. Discuss how the train passes through a variety of urban areas – city, suburbs and towns. Again, talk about the major differences.

A number of features of a railway line are introduced in the book, such as tunnels, cuttings and bridges. Look at the map symbols for these features. The concept of symbols can be hard for young children to grasp. A useful starting point may be to compare the bridleway on page 18 with the photograph. The photo shows what the symbol represents.

Throughout the book, and at each stage of the journey, a simple topological map shows the family's route. Talk about a journey familiar to the child. Identify significant features of the journey, then work together to design a topological map of the route.